BASS GUITAR PLAYING

EARLY GRADES

Preliminary Grade to Grade Two

Compiled by

Alan J Brown & Tony Skinner

on behalf of

RGT®

Registry of Guitar Tutors

www.RGT.org

British Library Cataloguing in Publication Data

Brown, Alan J & Skinner, Tony
Bass Guitar Playing – Early Grades

ISBN 1-898466-71-8

Published in Great Britain by

Registry Mews, 11 to 13 Wilton Road, Bexhill, East Sussex, TN40 1HY

Music and text typesetting by

Printed and bound in Great Britain
v.20110518

Contents

INTRODUCTION

This handbook is primarily intended to give advice and information to candidates taking the Preliminary, Grade 1 and Grade 2 examinations in Bass Guitar Playing. However, the information will undoubtedly be helpful to all bass guitarists, whether they intend to take the examination or not.

The handbook aims to aid the establishment of good musical and technical foundations. Although it can be used for independent study, it is best used as a supplement to individual or group tuition, and is not designed to replace the need for guidance from an experienced teacher.

To use this handbook to best effect it is essential that the general introductions to each chapter are carefully studied, in addition to the relevant sections for each grade.

In order to illustrate the information about scales, arpeggios and other bass patterns as clearly as possible to all players, regardless of experience, the book uses the Registry of Guitar Tutors' unique *Guitarograph* system.

The *Guitarograph* uses a combination of tablature, traditional notation and fingerboard diagram. These are explained individually below:

(1) Tablature

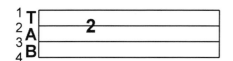

The horizontal lines represent the strings in descending order, as indicated. The numbers on the string lines refer to the frets at which the left-hand fingers should press. The above example therefore means: play on string 2 at fret 2.

(2) Bass clef notation

The lines and spaces of the bass clef indicate notes as follows:

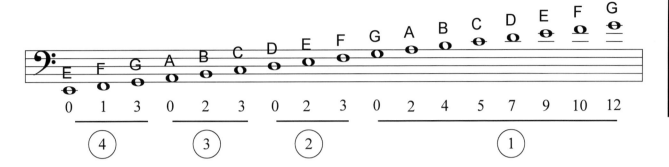

A sharp (#) before a note *raises* its pitch by a semitone, i.e. the note is played one fret higher.

A flat (♭) before a note *lowers* its pitch by a semitone, i.e. the note is played one fret lower.

In the above example, the circled numbers at the bottom refer to a string on which each note could be played. The other numbers refer to the fret on that string at which the note is to be found. The same note could be played on another string – so it is important to always refer to either the tablature or fingerboard diagram.

(3) Fingerboard diagram

Each horizontal line represents a string. The vertical lines represent the frets. Each fret is given a number in Roman numerals. Numbers on the horizontal lines indicate the left-hand finger to be used.

IV	III	II	I	
				E
				A
	3			D
				G

Play at the 3rd fret of the D string using the 3rd finger.

Guitarograph

All three previous methods are ways of illustrating the same information. In this handbook all are used in combination, using the *guitarograph*. This leaves no doubt as to what is required.

This example therefore means:
   play string 3 at fret 3 (tablature),
   play the note C (notation),
   use finger 3 (fingerboard diagram).

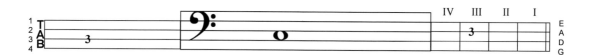

Above each *guitarograph* is a scale or arpeggio *formula*. This lists the letter names of the notes to be played, together with their *interval numbers*. The interval numbers refer to the position of the notes in comparison to the major scale with the same starting note.

For example:

C Major Scale

note names:	C	D	E	F	G	A	B	C
interval number:	1	2	3	4	5	6	7	8

Alternative positions and fingerings

When using the *guitarograph*, please remember that the *note names* given are definitive, that is, they cannot be changed. However, on the bass guitar, it is possible to play a note at more than one position on the fingerboard. For example, the note C given in the previous examples can also be played at the same pitch on string 4 at fret 8. This is called an alternative *position*. Nevertheless, you should normally play notes at the points indicated by the tablature and fingerboard diagrams, unless you are advised otherwise by your teacher. The reason can be shown by an example: in earlier grades, open string notes are often recommended to facilitate ease of playing; at higher grades, fretted notes are used more often to facilitate fingering of scales and patterns.

It is also possible to play the scales and patterns with fingers other than those indicated. There are various reasons why other fingers might be chosen. For example, on the bass guitar a major consideration is the size of a players hands, and the ability to stretch over several frets. The fingerings given in this handbook, although carefully chosen as being generally suitable, are only one possible recommended suggestion.

Please note that in the examinations you are allowed to use any alternative systematic fingering, *provided that this produces a good musical result.*

Tuning

The examiner will, upon request, offer an E or A note to tune to.

The use of an electronic tuner or other tuning aid, prior to or at the start of the examination, is permitted; candidates should be able to make any further adjustments, if required during the examination, unaided.

For examination purposes the bass guitar should be tuned to Standard Concert Pitch, that is A=440Hz. Candidates who normally adopt any other tuning should alter their tuning to Standard Pitch for the examination.

SECTION 1
Scales & Arpeggios

A maximum of 15 marks may be awarded in this section of the examination, with the emphasis on accurate, clear and even playing.

The scales and arpeggios required for each grade are listed on the following pages. The examiner will choose a selection of these and ask you to play them from memory. They should be played ascending and descending without a pause and without repeating the top note.

Choose a tempo at which you feel confident and maintain this evenly throughout – evenness and clarity are more important than speed for its own sake.

The choice of scales and arpeggios for Preliminary Grade aims to keep the left hand in one position, avoiding difficult position shifting at this early stage of learning. For Grades One and Two the "marker dot" system has been employed. The majority of bass guitars have marker dots on frets 3, 5 and 7, therefore scales and arpeggios have been chosen to start on these frets on either the E string or the A string. This avoids open strings and gives a good grounding in transpositional scale and arpeggio patterns which can later be moved around the fingerboard giving access to all keys.

Left-hand technique

Press the tips of the left-hand fingers as close to the frets as possible. This minimises both buzzes and the amount of pressure required, enabling you to play with a lighter, clearer, and hence more fluent, touch.

Try to keep all the left-hand fingers close to the fingerboard and have them hovering, ready to press, as this reduces the amount of movement required. Always have the left-hand fingers correctly spaced and ready in position before you begin to play.

Right-hand technique

You are free to use either your fingers or a plectrum for these examinations.

If you use a plectrum, alternate downstrokes with upstrokes. Grip the plectrum between the index finger and thumb, but be careful not to grip it too tightly as excessive gripping pressure can lead to muscular tension in the right hand and arm. Position the pick so that its point is about a half a centimetre beyond the fingertip. If too much of the plectrum extends beyond the finger a lack of control will result as it will flap around when striking the strings – this would consequently reduce fluency and accuracy.

If you choose to use your fingers, alternate between the index finger and middle finger, ensuring that each finger produces the same quality of sound. Keep your fingers close to the strings. The thumb may be rested on the E string whilst playing higher strings.

The *rest stroke* should be used for the majority of the time. To achieve the best results, rest your finger (either index or middle) on the string you wish to play. Pull towards the next lower string and when you have sufficient tension release the string, allowing the finger to fall onto the next lower string.

The more tension you put on the string (i.e. the harder you pull before you release) the louder the note produced. Try to avoid pressing the string into the guitar body or pulling it away. The best results are achieved by creating a *walking* effect – alternating the index and middle fingers.

For the purposes of the exam, volume should be of a medium strength. Loud enough to be clear and firm, but comfortable to play.

PRELIMINARY GRADE

Scales

The following one octave scales should be played ascending and descending from memory.

G Major

G	A	B	C	D	E	F♯	G
1	2	3	4	5	6	7	8

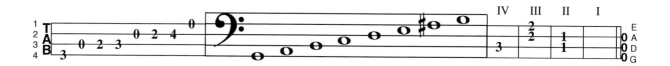

A Natural Minor

A	B	C	D	E	F	G	A
1	2	♭3	4	5	♭6	♭7	8

E Natural Minor

E	F♯	G	A	B	C	D	E
1	2	♭3	4	5	♭6	♭7	8

Arpeggios

The following one octave arpeggios should be played ascending and descending from memory.

A Major

A	C#	E	A
R	3	5	R

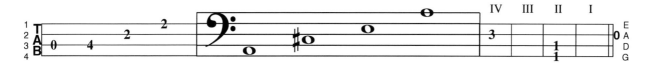

E Major

E	G#	B	E
R	3	5	R

G Major

G	B	D	G
R	3	5	R

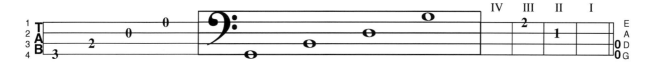

A Minor

A	C	E	A
R	♭3	5	R

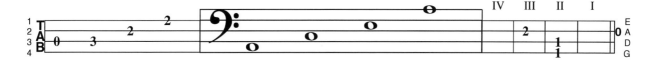

E Minor

E	G	B	E
R	♭3	5	R

11

GRADE ONE

Scales

The following one octave scales should be played ascending and descending from memory:

Major and Natural Minor in the keys of G, A, B, C, D, E.

Examples are given starting on G and C – showing the patterns for scales starting on the E string and the A string respectively. For the other scales required refer to the chart below detailing the starting string and fret for each scale.

scale/arpeggio	G	A	B	C	D	E
starting string	E	E	E	A	A	A
starting fret	3	5	7	3	5	7

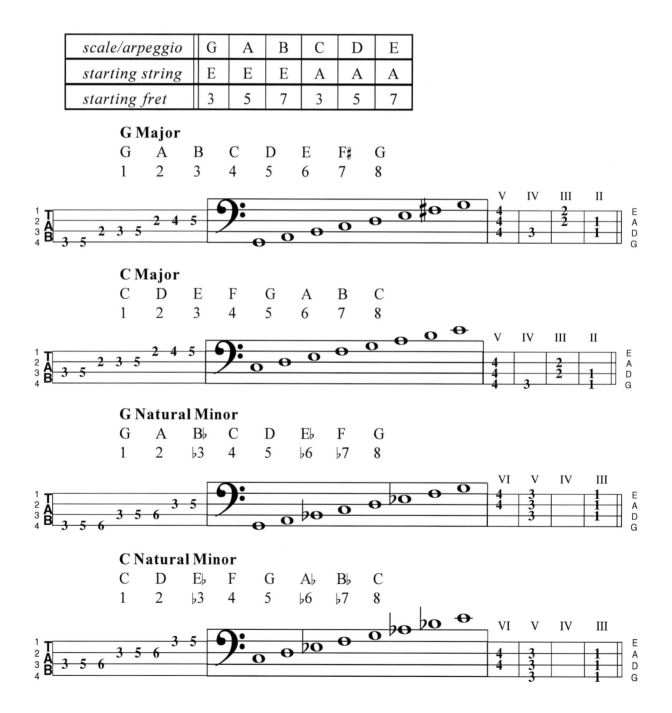

Arpeggios

The following one octave arpeggios should be played ascending and descending from memory:

Major and Minor with root notes of: G, A, B, C, D, E.

Examples are given starting on G and C – showing the patterns for arpeggios starting on the E string and the A string respectively. For the other arpeggios required refer to the chart in the scales section on the previous page which details the starting string and fret for each arpeggio.

G Major

G	B	D	G
R	3	5	R

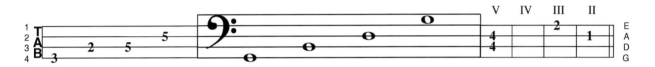

C Major

C	E	G	C
R	3	5	R

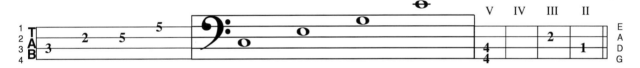

G Minor

G	B♭	D	G
R	♭3	5	R

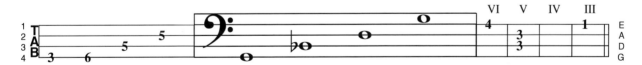

C Minor

C	E♭	G	C
R	♭3	5	R

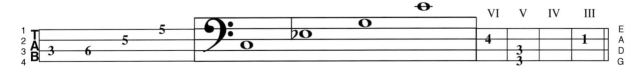

GRADE TWO

Scales

The following one octave scales should be played ascending and descending from memory:

Major, Natural Minor and Pentatonic Minor in the keys of G, A, B, C, D, E.

Examples are given starting on G and C – showing the patterns for scales starting on the E string and the A string respectively. For the other scales required refer to the chart below detailing the starting string and fret for each scale.

scale	G	A	B	C	D	E
starting string	E	E	E	A	A	A
starting fret	3	5	7	3	5	7

G Major

G	A	B	C	D	E	F♯	G
1	2	3	4	5	6	7	8

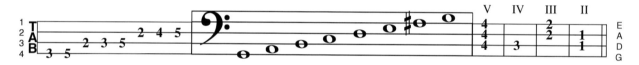

C Major

C	D	E	F	G	A	B	C
1	2	3	4	5	6	7	8

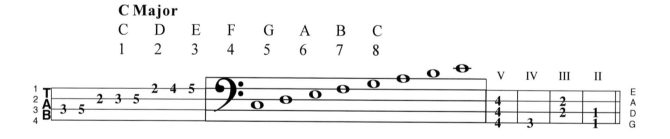

G Natural Minor

G	A	B♭	C	D	E♭	F	G
1	2	♭3	4	5	♭6	♭7	8

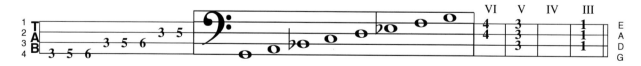

14

C Natural Minor

C	D	E♭	F	G	A♭	B♭	C
1	2	♭3	4	5	♭6	♭7	8

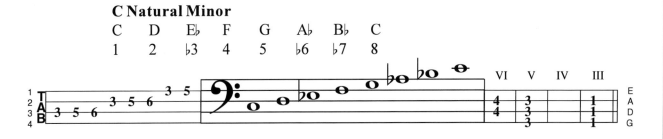

G Pentatonic Minor

G	B♭	C	D	F	G
1	♭3	4	5	♭7	8

C Pentatonic Minor

C	E♭	F	G	B♭	C
1	♭3	4	5	♭7	8

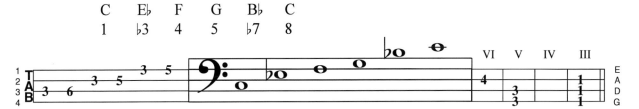

Arpeggios

The following one octave arpeggios should be played ascending and descending from memory:

Major 7th, Minor 7th and Dominant 7th with root notes of G, A, B, C, D, E.

Major and Minor in ALL keys.

Examples are given starting on G and C – showing the patterns for arpeggios starting on the E string and the A string respectively. For the other arpeggios required refer to the chart below detailing the starting string and fret for each arpeggio.

arpeggio	F♯/G♭	G	G♯/A♭	A	A♯/B♭	B	C	C♯/D♭	D	D♯/E♭	E	F
starting string	E	E	E	E	E	A	A	A	A	A	A	A
starting fret	2	3	4	5	6	2	3	4	5	6	7	8

15

G Major 7

G	B	D	F#	G
R	3	5	7	R

C Major 7

C	E	G	B	C
R	3	5	7	R

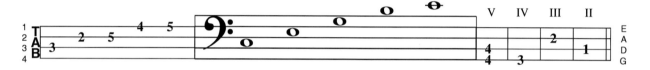

G Minor 7

G	B♭	D	F	G
R	♭3	5	♭7	R

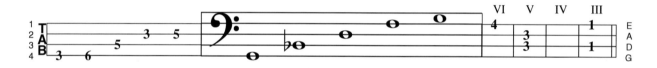

C Minor 7

C	E♭	G	B♭	C
R	♭3	5	♭7	R

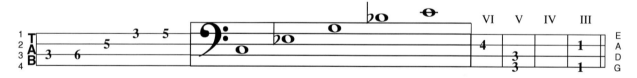

G 7

G	B	D	F	G
R	3	5	♭7	R

C 7

C	E	G	B♭	C
R	3	5	♭7	R

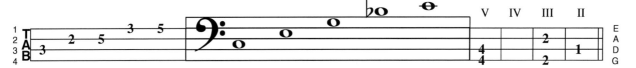

G Major

G	B	D	G
R	3	5	R

C Major

C	E	G	C
R	3	5	R

G Minor

G	B♭	D	G
R	♭3	5	R

C Minor

C	E♭	G	C
R	♭3	5	R

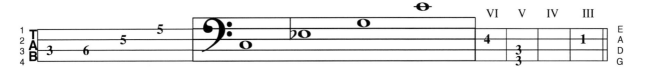

SECTION 2
Bass Patterns

A maximum of 24 marks may be awarded in this section of the examination.

The candidate should select two bass patterns from the four examples of the relevant grade given on the following pages. The candidate will then be shown a chord progression for one of the choices. The chosen bass pattern should be played over this sequence, transposing it for each chord. The chord progression should be played through twice. The second time the candidate may vary the pattern rhythmically, but should still follow the chord sequence and keep within the musical style. An indication of the style and suggested speed is given with each bass pattern.

Normally only one performance is required but, at the examiner's discretion, the candidate may be requested to play the second bass pattern over another chord sequence.

Marks will be awarded in this section for accuracy of pitch, security of timing and creativity. At these early grades, candidates should place most emphasis on the first two of these criteria.

The bass patterns and chords used in each sequence will be based on the requirements for Sections 1 and 3 of the relevant grade.

The following pages show the bass patterns in the key of C major or C minor, followed by examples of the type of progression to be expected in a selection of keys. Above the chord progression is the riff as it should be played for each chord. This is shown in both standard notation and tablature.

Please note that in the examination, candidates will be shown only a chord sequence. The bass pattern that is notated over each chord in this handbook is shown only for clarity and to facilitate the learning process. Such notation will NOT appear on the examination chord chart.

Above each bass pattern is given a broad indication of style together with a suggested metronome marking. These are a general guide to playing and some flexibility in interpretation is allowed.

A page of practice charts will be found for each grade. Candidates should practice playing the bass pattern over all the chords to be expected, in a variety of chord progressions, rather than merely practising the examples provided in this handbook.

18

PRELIMINARY GRADE

The chord sequence will contain some
of the following major or minor chords:

G, A, B, C, D, E.

1) Rock　♩ = 120

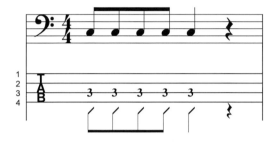

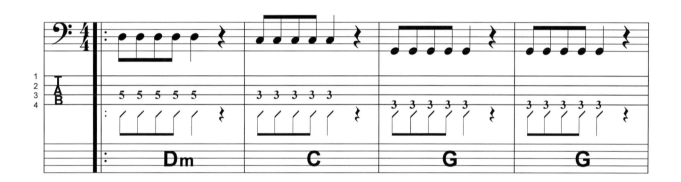

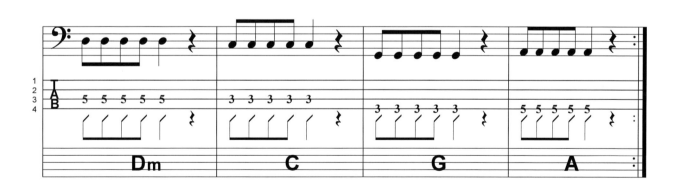

2) Ballad ♩ = 100

G   Am   C   D

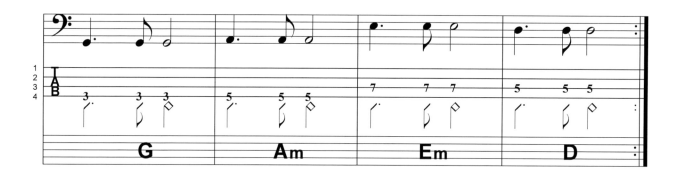

G   Am   Em   D

3) Dance   ♩ = 108

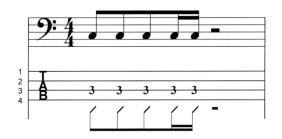

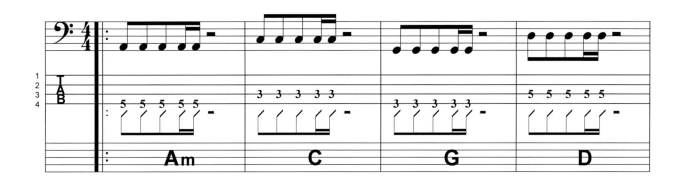

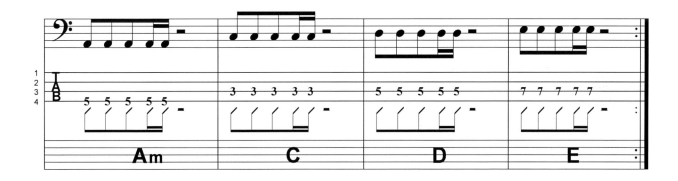

21

4) Soul ♩ = 96

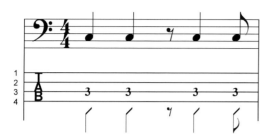

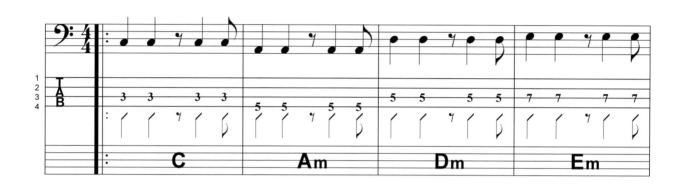

The chord charts below are *similar* to those presented to the candidate in the examination (i.e. without notation and tablature). They are given here as an aid to practice, with one progression for each bass pattern. Candidates are encouraged to practise each bass pattern over as many different chord progressions as possible.

1) Rock

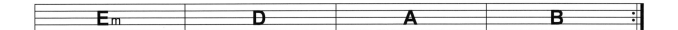

2) Ballad

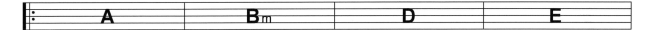

3) Dance

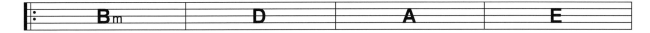

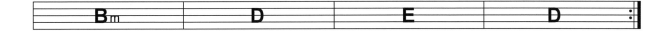

4) Soul

GRADE ONE

The chord sequence will contain some of the following major or minor chords:

G, A, B, C, D, E.

1) Heavy Rock   ♩ = 144

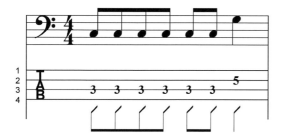

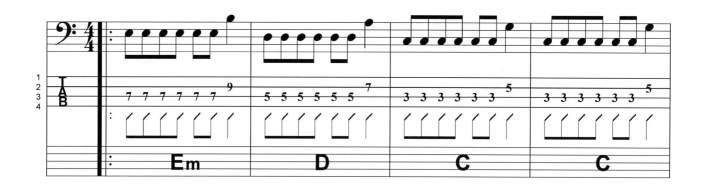

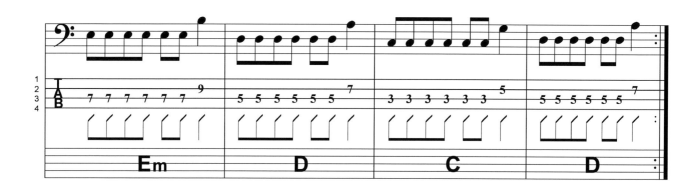

24

2) Pop   ♩ = 136

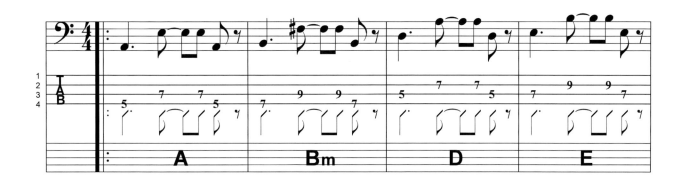

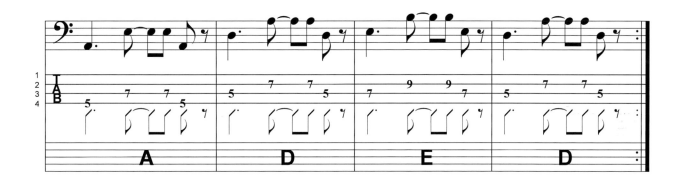

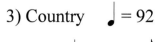

3) Country $\quad \quad = 92$

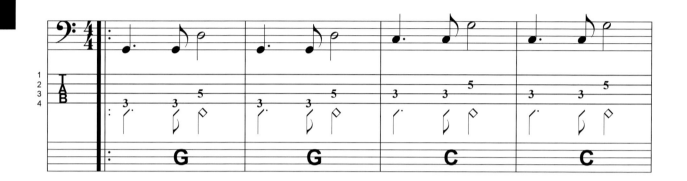

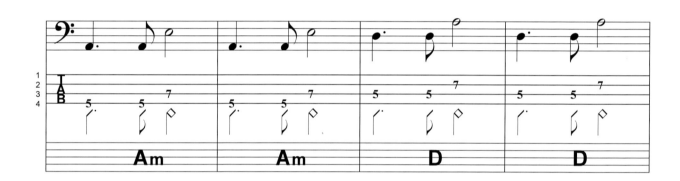

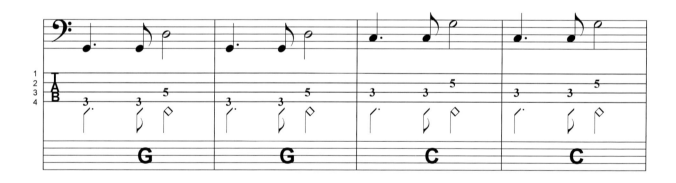

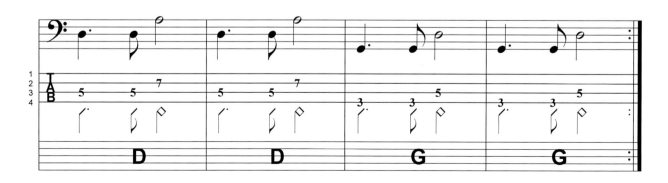

4) Funk ♩ = 92

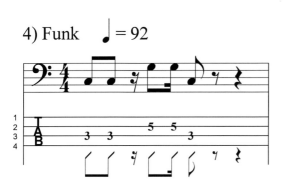

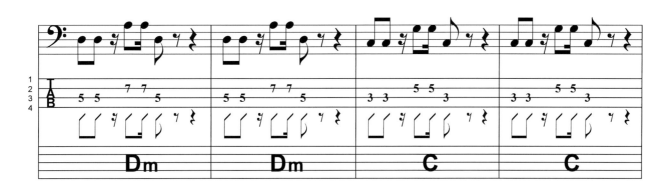

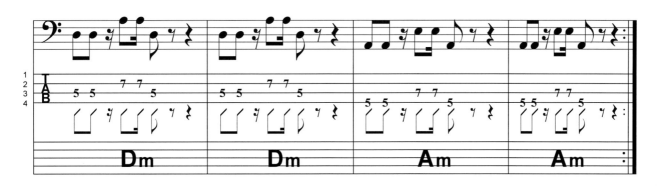

The chord charts below are *similar* to those presented to the candidate in the examination (i.e. without notation and tablature). They are given here as an aid to practice, with one progression for each bass pattern. Candidates are encouraged to practice each bass pattern over as many different chord progressions as possible.

1) Heavy Rock

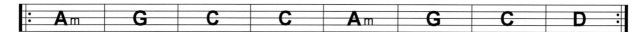

2) Pop

3) Country

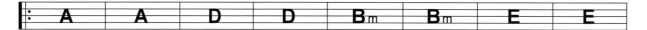

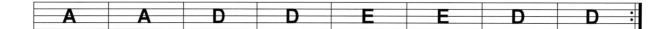

4) Funk

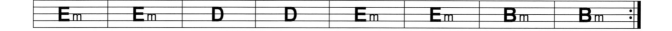

GRADE TWO

The chords used in this section are based on the arpeggio requirements for Grade 2 in Section 1 of this handbook.

The chord sequence may contain some of the following:

Major or minor chords in any key;

Major 7th, Minor 7th and Dominant 7th chords with root notes of G, A, B, C, D & E.

1) Reggae   ♩ = 120

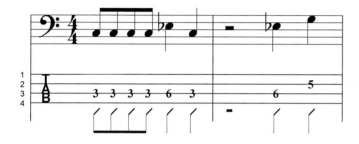

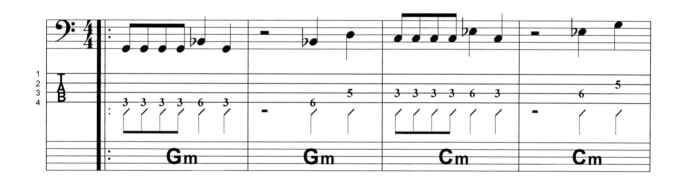

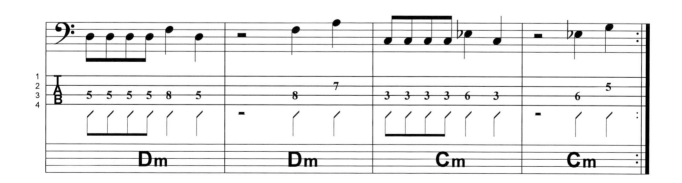

29

2) Pop ♩ = 144

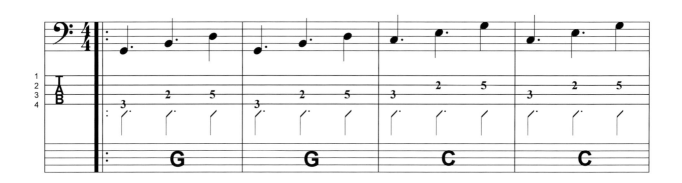

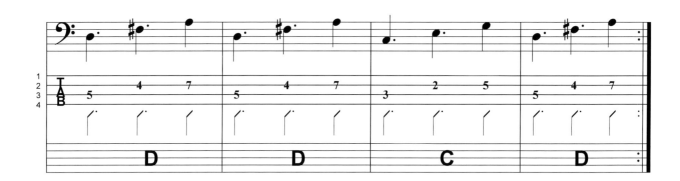

3) Electro ♩ = 100

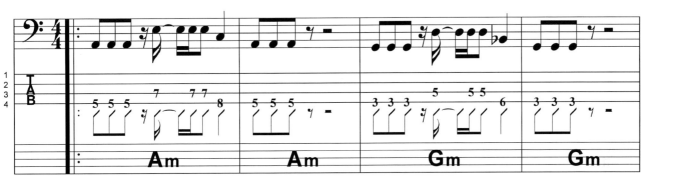

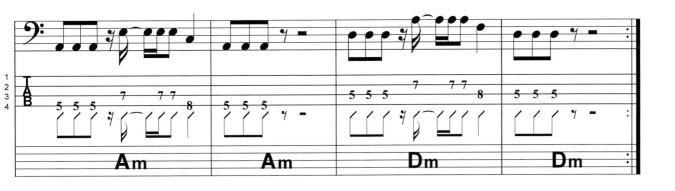

31

4) 60's Soul ♩ = 108

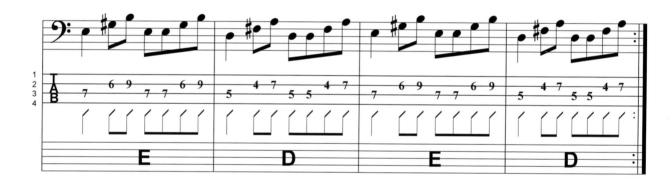

The chord charts below are *similar* to those presented to the candidate in the examination (i.e. without notation and tablature). They are given here as an aid to practice, with one progression for each bass pattern. Candidates are encouraged to practise each bass pattern over as many different chord progressions as possible.

1) Reggae

2) Pop

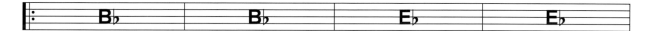

3) Electro

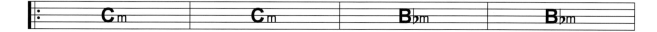

4) 60's Soul

SECTION 3
Performance

A maximum of 36 marks may be awarded in this section of the examination.

The candidate will be shown a chord sequence containing chords detailed for each grade on the following pages. The examiner will play through the sequence once on guitar for the candidate to hear. The examiner will then play the sequence a further two times and the candidate should improvise an appropriate bass line over the chords.

At the examiner's discretion, a second sequence may be given in a different style over which the candidate should again improvise an appropriate bass line after having heard the sequence once.

Marks will be awarded in this section for accuracy of pitch, security of timing, rhythmic inventiveness and creativity. At these early grades, candidates should place most emphasis on the first two of these criteria. Some examples of the type of sequence to be expected are shown for each grade on the following pages.

In the chord progressions, a lone upper case letter refers to a major chord (D = D Major) and a letter followed by a lower case 'm' refers to a minor chord (Dm = D Minor).

An upper case letter followed by a '7' refers to a dominant seventh chord, whilst 'm7' and 'Maj7' refer to minor seventh and major seventh respectively.

Improvising Bass Guitar
Books with CDs

RGT has produced a series of 'Improvising Bass Guitar' books and CDs to provide further advice, and to act as useful practice aids, for this section of the examination.

For more information on this series please see the inside rear cover or visit www.BooksForGuitar.com

PRELIMINARY GRADE

The chord sequence will contain some of the following major or minor chords:

G, A, B, C, D, E.

At this grade the candidate is not expected to play more than the root and possibly the 5th of each chord. The principle used is that of the "marker dot system" – the 3rd, 5th and 7th frets on the E and A string. By placing the first finger on the relevant note, the third finger (on the adjacent higher string) lies over the 5th of the chord. For notes on the A string, the 5th of the chord can also be played in a lower octave on the same fret on the adjacent lower string.

Some examples of the type of chart that may be presented at this grade are given below.

Note that at this grade the time signature is limited to $\frac{4}{4}$ time and there will be only one chord per bar. Some written indication regarding tempo and style will be given.

During the first playing of the sequence by the examiner, candidates should listen carefully to the way the chords are played in order to choose an appropriate style of bass line.

(i)   Moderate and light

$\frac{4}{4}$ | G | C | G | C | Am | D | Em | Em ‖

(ii)   Slow with feeling

$\frac{4}{4}$ | Am | Dm | Em | Dm | G | C | Dm | Am ‖

(iii) Lively

$\frac{4}{4}$ | C | Am | C | Am | Dm | Dm | G | G ‖

GRADE ONE

The chord sequence will contain some of the following major or minor chords:

G, A, B, C, D, E.

At this grade the candidate is expected to be fluent in playing the root and 5th of each chord and should demonstrate some ability in incorporating major or minor 3rds *when musically appropriate*. The principle used is that of the "marker dot system" – the 3rd, 5th and 7th frets on the E and A string. By placing the first finger on the relevant note, the third finger (on the adjacent higher string) lies over the 5th of the chord. For notes on the A string, the 5th of the chord can also be played in a lower octave on the same fret on the adjacent lower string.

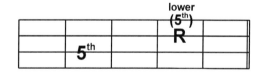

With the first finger on the root note, the fourth finger on the same string should lie over the minor 3rd.

Minor 3rd & 5th

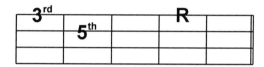

To play a major 3rd place your second finger on the root, enabling the major third to be played with the first finger on the next string up, one fret lower.

Major 3rd & 5th

Some examples of the type of chart that may be presented at this grade are given on the following page.

(i) Fairly slow and gentle in a ballad style

$\frac{4}{4}$ | A | A | D | Bm | A | E | A | A ‖

(ii) Funky, with movement

$\frac{4}{4}$ | Em | D | C | D | C | Am | G | D ‖

(iii) Moderately

$\frac{4}{4}$ | Am | Em | Dm | G | Am | Em | G | Am ‖

Note that at this grade the time signature is limited to $\frac{4}{4}$ time and there will be only one chord per bar. This does not imply that either four bass notes or one bass note should be played in each bar. The bass line should be determined by the style of the music and may vary between bars.

During the first playing of the sequence by the examiner, candidates should listen carefully to the way the chords are played in order to choose an appropriate style of bass line.

GRADE TWO

The chord sequence will contain chords taken from those required in Section 1 of the examination.

At this grade the candidate is expected to be fluent in playing the root and 5th of each chord, as well as the major or minor 3rd *if musically appropriate*. Some ability in incorporating major, minor and dominant 7ths, when musically appropriate, will also be expected. However, candidates should be careful not to 'overplay': there is certainly no need to include all the notes of the arpeggio over each chord - this could make the playing sound too busy and may distract from the overall musical style, limiting the development of a suitable musical 'feel' and 'groove'.

Some examples of the type of chart that may be presented at this grade are given below.

Note that at this grade the time signature is limited to $\frac{3}{4}$ or $\frac{4}{4}$ time and there will be only one chord per bar. This does not indicate the number of bass notes to be played in each bar; this should be determined by the style of the music and may vary between bars. Marks will be awarded for inventiveness of both notes used and rhythm played.

During the first playing of the sequence by the examiner, candidates should listen carefully to the way the chords are played in order to choose an appropriate style of bass line.

(i) In a light and easy style

| $\frac{4}{4}$ | G | Em | G | Em | Am | Am7 | D | D7 |

(ii) Not too slow

| $\frac{3}{4}$ | A | AMaj7 | D | DMaj7 | C♯m | Bm7 | E | E7 |

(iii) Bright and lively

| $\frac{4}{4}$ | C | Dm7 | Em7 | F | Am7 | G7 | C | C |

SECTION 4
Musicianship

A maximum of 10 marks may be awarded in this section of the examination.

Section 4 of the examination tests the candidate's knowledge of the notes being played, the instrument itself and the technical aspects of playing it. Whilst it is not necessary to have a detailed knowledge of the mechanism of the bass guitar at these early grades, candidates should be able to identify important parts of the instrument and be aware of how to adjust the controls. Also a basic knowledge of which notes are being played and some understanding of technique is important.

a) Musical knowledge

The candidate should be familiar with the notes in the scales and arpeggios required for the relevant grade (see Section 1 of this handbook). The examiner may ask the candidate to play a particular note on a particular string (such as "Play the note *A* on the *G* string"). In order to establish a solid musical foundation it is important that candidates are aware of the notes they are playing rather than merely duplicating finger patterns.

This section also tests the candidates knowledge of basic music theory. The ability to follow musical instructions such as repeat markings, dynamics, etc. is important when performing music and the candidate may be asked to demonstrate a particular term in addition to giving its definition. Specific requirements are given for each grade on the following pages.

b) Playing the bass guitar

This section covers the optimum methods of achieving clarity and fluency, with questions relating to both the left and right hands. Candidates should have a basic knowledge of both plectrum and finger styles irrespective of which they use during the examination. Specific requirements are given for each grade on the following pages.

c) Knowledge of the instrument

Candidates should have a basic general knowledge of the instrument. This section covers the anatomy of the bass guitar, including knowledge of the position and function of various items and familiarity with commonly used terms. Specific requirements are given for each grade on the following pages.

PRELIMINARY GRADE

a) Musical knowledge

The candidate should be able to name any note from the scales and arpeggios listed for Preliminary Grade in Section 1 of this handbook. The examiner will ask the candidate to play a particular note on a particular string (such as "Play the note *E* on the *D* string").

Candidates should be aware of the repeat mark. This consists of two dots and a double bar line at the start and end of the section to be repeated. (When the repeat is from the beginning of a piece the first set of dots is not always shown.) For example:

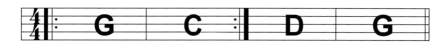

should be played as:

b) Playing the bass guitar

Candidates may be asked questions relating to the optimum positioning of the left-hand fingers, in particular how to obtain clear notes and avoid fret buzz. Section 1 of this handbook has details of left-hand technique, the most important aspect being keeping the left hand spread out and placing the tips of the fingers, rather than the pads, at the very edge of the frets. Candidates may be asked to demonstrate this on their bass guitar.

Section 1 of this handbook has details of right-hand technique, covering both plectrum and finger style.

c) Knowledge of the instrument

Candidates should be able to name the strings of the bass guitar:

4	3	2	1
E	A	D	G

The position of the machine heads, headstock, nut, bridge and saddles, pick-up, volume and tone controls (if appropriate) should be familiar and the candidate should be able to point to an item named by the examiner. The drawing below gives the positioning for most bass guitars – but do check your own instrument as some may vary.

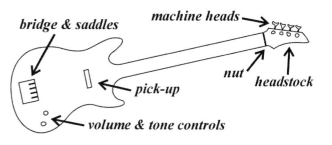

40

GRADE ONE

a) Musical knowledge

The candidate should be able to name any note from the scales and arpeggios listed for Grade One in Section 1 of this handbook. The examiner will ask the candidate to play a particular note on a particular string (such as "Play the note *C* on the *G* string").

At this grade the candidate should be able to explain the following repeat and dynamic markings. The candidate may also be asked to demonstrate dynamics with a question such as "Play the note *C* first *f* then *p*", or "Play four *C*s in the manner of this sign" (pointing to one of the dynamic markings).

Repeat marks

Passages to be repeated are indicated by two dots and a double bar line at the start and end of the particular section.

(When the repeat is from the beginning of a piece the first set of dots is not always shown.)

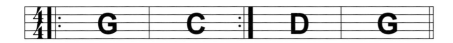 should be played as:

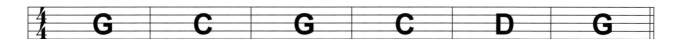

Dynamic Markings

These indicate the changes in volume to be made.

> *p*   – play softly
>
> *f*   – play strongly
>
>   – become louder
>
>   – become softer

Candidates may be given a chord sequence consisting of up to four bars with one chord per bar. The chart will contain dynamic and repeat markings. The chord sequence should be played through using four root notes per bar and incorporating the performance indications. An example of the type of chart to be expected is given below.

MUSICIANSHIP

b) Playing the bass guitar

Candidates may be asked questions relating to the optimum positioning of the left-hand fingers, in particular how to obtain clear notes and avoid fret buzz. Section 1 of this handbook has details of left-hand technique, the most important aspect being keeping the left hand spread out and placing the tips of the fingers, rather than the pads, at the very edge of the frets.

Take care not to over-grip with the left-hand thumb on the back of the neck as this will cause muscle fatigue and tend to limit the freedom of the thumb to move. It is essential that the left-hand thumb is allowed to move freely when changing positions. If the thumb remains static this restricts the optimum positioning of the fingers which may result in unnecessary left hand stretching and consequent loss of fluency. Also be aware that for the left-hand thumb to move freely the wrist, elbow and shoulder must be flexible and relaxed. Try to ensure that this is not inhibited by your standing or sitting position.

With regard to the right hand: Plectrum strokes should alternate between down and up strokes and, in finger style, index and middle fingers should alternate to facilitate fluency and speed. Section 1 of this handbook has details of right-hand technique, covering both plectrum and finger style.

In addition to answering questions, the candidate should be able to demonstrate any of the above if requested to do so.

c) Knowledge of the instrument

Candidates should have a basic general knowledge of the instrument. In particular:

i) Variations in tone achieved by changing the right hand position. For instance a brighter clearer attack will be produced when playing close to the bridge, whereas a more mellow tone is produced as you move towards the fingerboard.

ii) The function of the machine heads. These are "normally" positioned by the headstock of the guitar. Each string has its own machine head (or turning head) which, when rotated, increases or reduces the tension exerted on that string, thereby raising or lowering its pitch. By carefully adjusting all of these the bass guitar can be brought into tune.

iii) The meaning of common terms such as:

Action – the distance between the strings and the frets. This determines the ease of fretting notes.

Marker dots – the dots or blocks inlaid into the face and/or side of the fingerboard to give the location of certain frets. These normally include frets 3, 5, 7, 9 & 12.

GRADE TWO

a) Musical knowledge

The candidate should be able to name any note on any string up to, and including, the twelfth fret. This includes all the notes from the scales and arpeggios required for Grade Two. The examiner will ask the candidate to play a particular note on a particular string (such as "Play the note E on the G string").

The chart below shows all the notes on all four strings for the first twelve frets.

At this grade the candidate should be able to explain the repeat and dynamic markings detailed below. The candidate may also be asked to demonstrate dynamics with a question such as "Play the note C first f then p", or "Play four Cs in the manner of this sign" (pointing to one of the dynamic markings).

12	11	10	9	8	7	6	5	4	3	2	1	fret
E	D#/E♭	D	C#/D♭	C	B	A#/B♭	A	G#/A♭	G	F#/G♭	F	E string
A	G#/A♭	G	F#/G♭	F	E	D#/E♭	D	C#/D♭	C	B	A#/B♭	A string
D	C#/D♭	C	B	A#/B♭	A	G#/A♭	G	F#/G♭	F	E	D#/E♭	D string
G	F#/G♭	F	E	D#/E♭	D	C#/D♭	C	B	A#/B♭	A	G#/A♭	G string

Repeat marks

Passages to be repeated are indicated by two dots and a double bar line at the start and end of the particular section. (When the repeat is from the beginning of a piece the first set of dots is not always shown.) For example:

should be played as:

43

1st and 2nd time endings

Bars marked with a 1. are included in the first playing but omitted on the repeat playing and replaced with the bars marked 2.

For example:

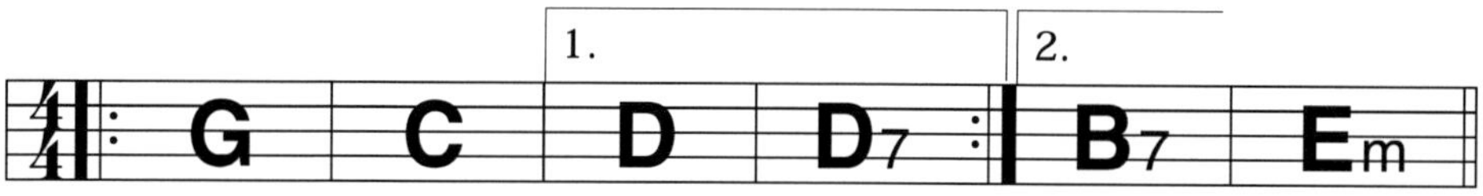

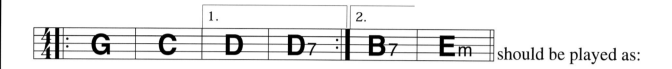

should be played as:

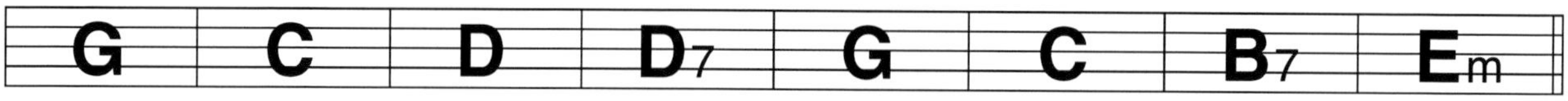

Dynamic Markings

These indicate the changes in volume to be made.

p – play softly

f – play strongly

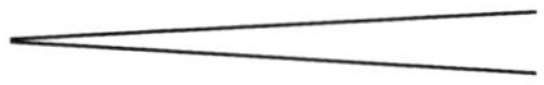 – become louder

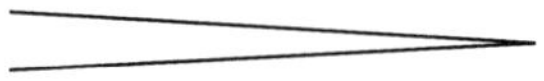 – become softer

Candidates may be given a chord sequence consisting of up to four bars with one chord per bar. The chart will contain dynamic and repeat markings. The chord sequence should be played through using four root notes per bar and incorporating the performance indications. An example of the type of chart to be expected is given below.

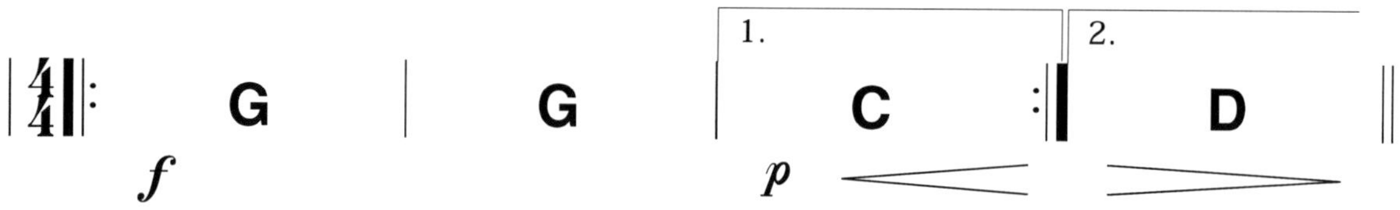

b) Playing the bass guitar

Candidates may be asked questions relating to the optimum positioning of the left-hand fingers, in particular how to obtain clear notes and avoid fret buzz. Section 1 of this handbook has details of left-hand technique, the most important aspect being to place the tips of the fingers, rather than the pads, at the very edge of the frets.

Take care not to over-grip with the left-hand thumb on the back of the neck as this will cause muscle fatigue and tend to limit the freedom of the thumb to move. It is essential that the left-hand thumb is allowed to move freely when changing positions. If the thumb remains static this restricts the optimum positioning of the fingers which may result in unnecessary left hand stretching and consequent loss of fluency. Also be aware that for the left-hand thumb to move freely the wrist, elbow and shoulder must be flexible and relaxed. Try to ensure that this is not inhibited by your standing or sitting position.

With regard to the right hand. Plectrum strokes should alternate between down and up strokes and, in finger style, index and middle fingers should alternate to facilitate fluency and speed. Section 1 of this handbook has details of right-hand technique, covering both plectrum and finger style.

In addition to answering questions, the candidate should be able to demonstrate any of the above.

c) *Knowledge of the instrument*

Candidates should have a good basic general knowledge of the bass. In particular:

i) Variations in tone achieved by changing the right hand position. For instance a brighter clearer attack will be produced when playing close to the bridge, whereas a more mellow tone is produced as you move towards the fingerboard.

When applicable, a demonstration of the candidate's working knowledge of the tone controls and pick-up selector may be requested.

ii) The function of the machine heads. These are normally positioned by the headstock of the guitar. Each string has its own machine head (or turning head) which, when rotated, increases or reduces the tension exerted on that string, thereby raising or lowering its pitch. By carefully adjusting all of these the bass guitar can be brought into tune.

iii) The meaning of terms such as:

Action – the distance between the strings and the frets. This determines the ease of fretting notes.

Marker dots – the dots or blocks inlaid into the face and/or side of the fingerboard to give the location of certain frets. These normally include frets 3, 5, 7, 9 & 12.

The nut – a slotted piece of material (normally plastic or brass) situated at the head end of the fingerboard. The strings lie in the grooves of the nut.

The saddle – the seat upon which the string rests at the body end of the bass guitar. It is from this point that the vibrating section of the string starts.

SECTION 5
Aural Assessment

A maximum of 15 marks may be awarded in this section of the examination.

This section of the examination tests the aural abilities of the candidate. It consists of five sections as detailed below. Three or more sections may be tested in the examination at the discretion of the examiner, but the candidate is expected to be competent in all five.

a) Repetition of rhythms

The examiner will twice play on a single note a rhythmic pattern (examples of which are given for each grade on the following pages). The candidate should then attempt to reproduce this rhythm by either clapping or playing on any note.

b) Repetition of phrases

The candidate will be asked to look away whilst the examiner plays a four beat phrase. The phrase will be taken from one of the required scales from the appropriate grade (see Section 1 of this handbook). The candidate will be told which scale is being used, and the root note will be played. The examiner will play the phrase twice before the candidate makes a first attempt to reproduce the phrase. If required, the examiner will play the phrase one further time prior to the candidate's second attempt. In order to simulate circumstances which commonly occur

for bass players in a band situation, the examiner will play the phrase on the guitar and the candidate is expected to reproduce it one octave lower on the bass guitar. Examples of the type of phrase which will occur at each grade are given on the following pages.

c) Beating of time

The examiner will play a four bar phrase twice. During the second playing the candidate should tap or clap the main pulse, accenting the first beat of the bar. An example is given for each grade on the following pages.

d) Harmony test

This section tests recognition of chord types. The examiner will play the test on guitar whilst the candidate looks away. Details of the requirements for each grade are given on the following pages.

e) Pitch test

This test will be played by the examiner on the candidate's bass guitar. In contrast to d) above, which tests a general awareness of chords and chord types, this test is related to individual notes in the range actually being played on the bass guitar. The requirements for each grade are given on the following pages.

PRELIMINARY GRADE

a) Repetition of rhythms

The examiner will twice play on a single note a two bar rhythm in ⁴⁄₄ time: bar 1 containing 4 quavers and 2 crotchets, bar 2 containing a semibreve.

The candidate should then attempt to reproduce this rhythm by either clapping or playing. Some examples of the type of rhythm are given below.

b) Repetition of phrases

The phrase given at this grade will consist of adjacent notes taken from a scale listed for Preliminary Grade in Section 1 of this handbook. The phrase may consist of crotchets and quavers, but quavers will only occur on notes of the same pitch. Some examples of the type of phrases are shown on the following page.

Examiner plays:

Candidate plays:

Taken from A Natural Minor Scale

Examiner plays:

Candidate plays:

Taken from G Major Scale

Examiner plays:

Candidate plays:

Taken from E Natural Minor Scale

c) Beating of time

The examiner will play a four bar phrase in $\frac{4}{4}$ time using only minims, crotchets and quavers. During the second playing the candidate should tap or clap the main pulse, accenting the first beat of the bar. An example is given below.

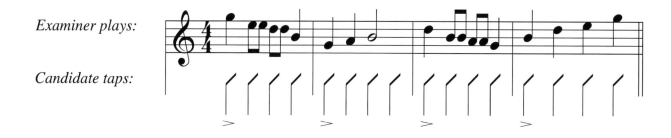

Examiner plays:

Candidate taps:

d) Harmony tests

Whilst the candidate looks away, the examiner will play a few bars of music containing either two major chords or two minor chords. The candidate will then be asked whether the sequence contained major or minor chords.

It may be helpful to note that major chords tend to give the effect of being bright, cheerful and strong, whereas minor chords leave an impression of being more mellow, sombre and dark.

Examples:

(i)   ‖ A | E | A | E . A . ‖   —   *major*

(ii)   ‖ Em | Am | Em | Am . Em . ‖—   *minor*

e) Pitch tests

The examiner will play two diatonic notes consecutively, which will be no more than a perfect fifth apart. The candidate will then be asked to identify which one was the lower or higher note. It will be found easier to answer this question correctly if the candidate sings or hums the two notes either aloud or in the head.

Example:

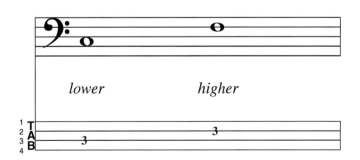

GRADE ONE

a) Repetition of rhythms

The examiner will twice play on a single note a two bar rhythm in ¾ time – containing only minims, crotchets and quavers.

The candidate should then attempt to reproduce this rhythm by either clapping, tapping or playing. Some examples of the type of rhythm are given below.

b) Repetition of phrases

The phrase given at this grade will consist of adjacent notes taken from a scale listed for Grade One in Section 1 of this handbook. The phrase may consist of crotchets, quavers and semiquavers, but semiquavers will only occur on notes of the same pitch. Some examples of the type of phrases are shown on the following page.

Examiner plays:

Candidate plays:

Taken from
A Natural Minor Scale

Taken from
G Major Scale

Taken from
D Natural Minor Scale

Taken from
E Major Scale

c) Beating of time

The examiner will play a four bar phrase in ⁴⁄₄ time using only minims, crotchets, quavers and semiquavers. During the second playing the candidate should tap or clap the main pulse, accenting the first beat of the bar. An example is given below.

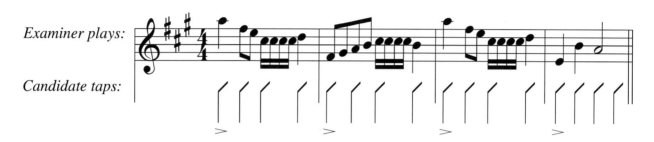

d) Harmony tests

Whilst the candidate looks away, the examiner will twice play either a single major chord or a single minor chord. The candidate will be asked to identify whether the chord was major or minor.

Examples:

(i)   ‖   D   ‖   *major*

(ii)   ‖   Am   ‖   *minor*

e) Pitch tests

The examiner will play the note of C followed by another note taken from the first five notes of the C Major Scale. The candidate will then be asked to identify the second note either by letter name or interval number.

It will be easier to remember the sound of these intervals if at first each one is related to the start of a familiar tune or riff. For example, the following traditional tunes start with a perfect fourth – Amazing Grace, Auld Lang Syne, Away in a Manger.

GRADE TWO

a) Repetition of rhythms

The examiner will twice play on a single note a four bar rhythm in either ¾ or ⁴₄ time containing only minims, crotchets or quavers – except for the last bar, which will contain only one long note. The candidate should then attempt to reproduce this rhythm by either clapping or playing. Some examples of the type of rhythm are given below. Note that the first and third bars will be identical.

b) Repetition of phrases

The phrase given at this grade will consist of notes within a range of one octave taken from a scale listed for Grade Two in Section 1 of this handbook. The phrase will start on the root note and will contain three other crotchet notes. Some examples of the type of phrases are shown below.

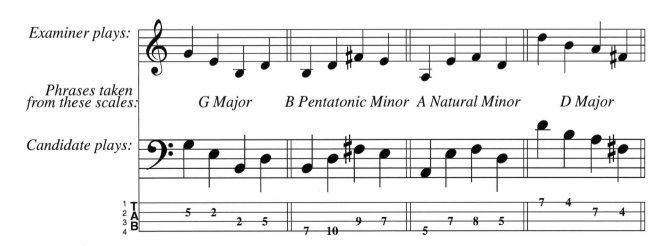

53

c) Beating of time

The examiner will play a four bar phrase in $\frac{3}{4}$ or $\frac{4}{4}$ time which may include dotted notes and semiquavers. During the second playing the candidate should tap or clap the main pulse, accenting the first beat of the bar. An example is given below.

Examiner plays:

Candidate taps:

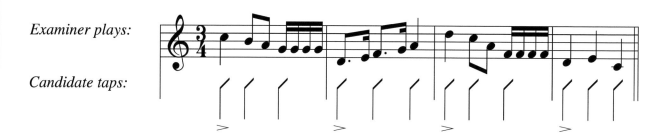

d) Harmony tests

Whilst the candidate looks away, the examiner will play a few bars of music containing exclusively either minor 7th, dominant 7th or major 7th chords. The candidate will then be asked which type of chord was used.

Examples:

(i)   ‖ Am7 | Dm7 | Am7 . Dm7 . | Am7 ‖

(ii)   ‖ A7 | D7 | A7 . D7 . | A7 ‖

(iii)   ‖ Amaj7 | Dmaj7 | Amaj7 . Dmaj7 . | Amaj7 ‖

e) Pitch tests

The candidate will be asked to identify any note of the one octave Major Scale of C or G. The examiner will first state the key then play the key note, followed by any other note of the scale. The candidate should identify the second note either by letter name or interval number.

| C to D | C to E | C to F | C to G | C to A | C to B | C to C |
| Major 2nd | Major 3rd | Perfect 4th | Perfect 5th | Major 6th | Major 7th | Octave |

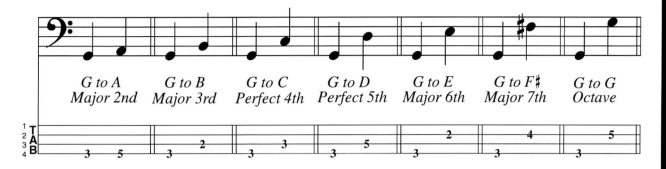

It will be easier to remember the sound of these intervals if at first each one is related to the start of a familiar tune or riff. For example, the following tunes start with a perfect fourth – Amazing Grace, Auld Lang Syne, Away in a Manger.

Conclusion

Examination tips

1. Many of the musical examples given in this handbook may be presented in different keys during the examination. Practising in a range of keys should be considered as essential examination preparation.

2. In the final weeks leading up to the examination practice should focus on weak areas, but do not neglect the main 'Bass Patterns' and 'Performance' sections as these carry the majority of the marks.

3. During the examination, the examiner's numerous questions and tests may seem daunting at first, but these are never designed to 'catch you out'. The breadth of the questions and tests are purely aimed at allowing you the opportunity to display the range and depth of the musical abilities and knowledge that you have developed. Although, as well as complimenting your achievements, the examiner will offer written advice on any areas in which you need to devote more study.

4. During the examination, the examiner will need to make written notes about your performance. This enables the examiner to compile a helpful examination report, which will be forwarded to you after the examination. So do not be put off if you see the examiner 'reach for a pen' – it does not necessarily mean that an error has been noted, it is just as likely that the examiner is noting a positive comment about some aspect of the performance.

5. Try to dispel any nerves by viewing the examination not as a daunting test, but rather as a positive opportunity to demonstrate your musical skills and talents, and to have these formally recognised and rewarded.

Entering for the examination

After studying this handbook, you may wish to enter for one of the examinations. Please ensure you are familiar with the general regulations and current requirements by reading the current Examination Syllabus and the Bass Guitar Exam Information Booklet – both downloadable from www.RGT.org

UK candidates may enter and pay for the examinations online via the RGT website, www.RGT.org, using the unique entry codes printed below *or* by using the entry forms in the back of this book.

To enter online visit **www.RGT.org** where entry fees can be paid by credit or debit card. In order to enter online you will need to input your unique and confidential examination entry code for the appropriate grade:

Preliminary Grade Online Entry Code: BP-7271-BR

Grade One Online Entry Code: BA-6140-BS

Grade Two Online Entry Code: BB-7494-BT

Keep these codes confidential, as each one can only be used once.

Overseas candidates cannot enter for examinations online and should use the entry forms within this book.

Registry of Guitar Tutors

Registry of Guitar Tutors
Registry Mews, 11 to 13 Wilton Road,
Bexhill, East Sussex, TN40 1HY

Tel: 01424 22 22 22   Fax: 01424 21 32 21

Email: office@RGT.org

Bass players – go surfing ...

... the Registry of Guitar Tutors' recommended website for bass guitar books and educational material

EXAMINATION ENTRY FORM
BASS GUITAR
PRELIMINARY GRADE

RGT
Registry of Guitar Tutors

ONLINE ENTRY – AVAILABLE FOR UK CANDIDATES ONLY

For **UK candidates**, entries and payments can be made online at www.RGT.org, using your unique and confidential examination entry code shown on page 57 of this book.

You will be able to pay the entry fee by credit or debit card at a secure payment page on the RGT website.

Once you have entered online, you should sign this form overleaf. **You must bring this signed form to your exam and hand it to the examiner in order to be admitted to the exam room.**

If NOT entering online, please complete BOTH sides of this form and return to the address overleaf.

SESSION (Spring/Summer/Winter): _____ YEAR: _____

Dates/times NOT available: _____

Note: Only name *specific* dates (and times on those dates) when it would be <u>absolutely impossible</u> for you to attend due to important prior commitments (such as pre-booked overseas travel) which cannot be cancelled. We will then endeavour to avoid scheduling an exam session in your area on those dates. In fairness to all other candidates in your area, **only list dates on which it would be impossible for you to attend.** An entry form that blocks out unreasonable periods may be returned. (Exams may be held on any day of the week including, but not exclusively, weekends. Exams may be held within or outside of the school term.)

Candidate Details: *Please write as clearly as possible using BLOCK CAPITALS*

Candidate Name (as to appear on certificate): _____

Address: _____

_____ Postcode: _____

Tel. No. (day): _____ (mobile): _____

IMPORTANT: Please take care to write your email address below *as clearly as possible* as your exam entry acknowledgement and your exam appointment details will be sent to this email address.

Email:_____
Where an email address is provided your exam correspondence will be sent by email only, and not by post. This will ensure your exam correspondence will reach you sooner.

Teacher Details *(if applicable)*

Teacher Name (as to appear on certificate): _____

RGT Tutor Code (if applicable): _____

Address: _____

_____ Postcode: _____

Tel. No. (day): _____ (mobile): _____

Email:_____

BASS GUITAR – RGT Official Entry Form

The standard LCM entry form is NOT valid for Bass Guitar exam entries.
Entry to the examination is only possible via this original form.
Photocopies of this form will not be accepted under *any* circumstances.

- Completion of this entry form is an agreement to comply with the current syllabus requirements and conditions of entry published at www.RGT.org. Where candidates are entered for examinations by a teacher, parent or guardian that person hereby takes responsibility that the candidate is entered in accordance with the current syllabus requirements and conditions of entry.

- If you are being taught by an *RGT registered* tutor, please hand this completed form to your tutor and request him/her to administer the entry on your behalf.

- For candidates with special needs, a letter giving details should be attached.

Examination Fee: £_____   Late Entry Fee (if applicable): £_____

Total amount submitted: £_____

Cheques or postal orders should be made payable to Registry of Guitar Tutors.

Details of conditions of entry, entry deadlines and examination fees are obtainable from the RGT website: www.RGT.org

Once an entry has been accepted, entry fees cannot be refunded.

CANDIDATE INFORMATION (UK Candidates only)

In order to meet our obligations in monitoring the implementation of equal opportunities policies, UK candidates are required to supply the information requested below. *The information provided will in no way whatsoever influence the marks awarded during the examination.*

Date of birth: _____ Age: _____ Gender – please circle: male / female

Ethnicity (please enter 2 digit code from chart below): _____ Signed: _____

ETHNIC ORIGIN CLASSIFICATIONS (If you prefer not to say, write '17' in the space above.)

White: **01 British**   **02 Irish**   **03 Other white background**

Mixed: **04 White & black Caribbean**   **05 White & black African**   **06 White & Asian**   **07 Other mixed background**

Asian or Asian British: **08 Indian**   **09 Pakistani**   **10 Bangladeshi**   **11 Other Asian background**

Black or Black British: **12 Caribbean**   **13 African**   **14 Other black background**

Chinese or Other Ethnic Group: **15 Chinese**   **16 Other**   **17 Prefer not to say**

I understand and accept the current syllabus regulations and conditions of entry for this examination as specified on the RGT website.

Signed by candidate (if aged 18 or over) _____ Date _____

If candidate is under 18, this form should be signed by a parent/guardian/teacher (circle which applies):

Signed _____ Name _____ Date _____

UK ENTRIES

See overleaf for details of how to enter online OR return this form to:
Registry of Guitar Tutors, Registry Mews, 11 to 13 Wilton Road, Bexhill-on-Sea, E. Sussex, TN40 1HY
(If you have submitted your entry online do NOT post this form, instead you need to sign it above and hand it to the examiner on the day of your exam.)
To contact the RGT office telephone 01424 222222 or Email office@RGT.org

NON-UK ENTRIES

To locate the address within your country that entry forms should be sent to, and to view exam fees in your currency, visit the RGT website **www.RGT.org** and navigate to the 'RGT Worldwide' section.

EXAMINATION ENTRY FORM
BASS GUITAR
GRADE ONE

RGT — Registry of Guitar Tutors

ONLINE ENTRY – AVAILABLE FOR UK CANDIDATES ONLY

For **UK candidates**, entries and payments can be made online at www.RGT.org, using your unique and confidential examination entry code shown on page 57 of this book.

You will be able to pay the entry fee by credit or debit card at a secure payment page on the RGT website.

Once you have entered online, you should sign this form overleaf. **You must bring this signed form to your exam and hand it to the examiner in order to be admitted to the exam room.**

If NOT entering online, please complete BOTH sides of this form and return to the address overleaf.

SESSION (Spring/Summer/Winter): _____ YEAR: _____

Dates/times NOT available: _____

Note: Only name *specific* dates (and times on those dates) when it would be *absolutely impossible* for you to attend due to important prior commitments (such as pre-booked overseas travel) which cannot be cancelled. We will then endeavour to avoid scheduling an exam session in your area on those dates. In fairness to all other candidates in your area, **only list dates on which it would be impossible for you to attend.** An entry form that blocks out unreasonable periods may be returned. (Exams may be held on any day of the week including, but not exclusively, weekends. Exams may be held within or outside of the school term.)

Candidate Details: *Please write as clearly as possible using BLOCK CAPITALS*

Candidate Name (as to appear on certificate): _____

Address: _____

_____ Postcode: _____

Tel. No. (day): _____ (mobile): _____

IMPORTANT: Please take care to write your email address below *as clearly as possible* as your exam entry acknowledgement and your exam appointment details will be sent to this email address.

Email: _____

Where an email address is provided your exam correspondence will be sent by email only, and not by post. This will ensure your exam correspondence will reach you sooner.

Teacher Details *(if applicable)*

Teacher Name (as to appear on certificate): _____

RGT Tutor Code (if applicable): _____

Address: _____

_____ Postcode: _____

Tel. No. (day): _____ (mobile): _____

Email: _____

BASS GUITAR – RGT Official Entry Form

The standard LCM entry form is NOT valid for Bass Guitar exam entries.
Entry to the examination is only possible via this original form.
Photocopies of this form will not be accepted under *any* circumstances.

- Completion of this entry form is an agreement to comply with the current syllabus requirements and conditions of entry published at www.RGT.org. Where candidates are entered for examinations by a teacher, parent or guardian that person hereby takes responsibility that the candidate is entered in accordance with the current syllabus requirements and conditions of entry.

- If you are being taught by an *RGT registered* tutor, please hand this completed form to your tutor and request him/her to administer the entry on your behalf.

- For candidates with special needs, a letter giving details should be attached.

Examination Fee: £_____ Late Entry Fee (if applicable): £_____

Total amount submitted: £_____

Cheques or postal orders should be made payable to Registry of Guitar Tutors.

Details of conditions of entry, entry deadlines and examination fees are obtainable from the RGT website: www.RGT.org

Once an entry has been accepted, entry fees cannot be refunded.

CANDIDATE INFORMATION (UK Candidates only)

In order to meet our obligations in monitoring the implementation of equal opportunities policies, UK candidates are required to supply the information requested below. *The information provided will in no way whatsoever influence the marks awarded during the examination.*

Date of birth: _____ Age: _____ Gender – please circle: male / female

Ethnicity (please enter 2 digit code from chart below): _____ Signed: _____

ETHNIC ORIGIN CLASSIFICATIONS (If you prefer not to say, write '17' in the space above.)

White: **01 British**   **02 Irish**   **03 Other white background**

Mixed: **04 White & black Caribbean**   **05 White & black African**   **06 White & Asian**   **07 Other mixed background**

Asian or Asian British: **08 Indian**   **09 Pakistani**   **10 Bangladeshi**   **11 Other Asian background**

Black or Black British: **12 Caribbean**   **13 African**   **14 Other black background**

Chinese or Other Ethnic Group: **15 Chinese**   **16 Other**   **17 Prefer not to say**

I understand and accept the current syllabus regulations and conditions of entry for this examination as specified on the RGT website.

Signed by candidate (if aged 18 or over) _____ Date _____

If candidate is under 18, this form should be signed by a parent/guardian/teacher (circle which applies):

Signed _____ Name_____ Date_____

UK ENTRIES

See overleaf for details of how to enter online OR return this form to:
Registry of Guitar Tutors, Registry Mews, 11 to 13 Wilton Road, Bexhill-on-Sea, E. Sussex, TN40 1HY
(If you have submitted your entry online do NOT post this form, instead you need to sign it above and hand it to the examiner on the day of your exam.)
To contact the RGT office telephone 01424 222222 or Email office@RGT.org

NON-UK ENTRIES

To locate the address within your country that entry forms should be sent to, and to view exam fees in your currency, visit the RGT website **www.RGT.org** and navigate to the 'RGT Worldwide' section.

EXAMINATION ENTRY FORM
BASS GUITAR
GRADE TWO

RGT The Specialist in Guitar Education
Registry of Guitar Tutors

ONLINE ENTRY – AVAILABLE FOR UK CANDIDATES ONLY

For **UK candidates**, entries and payments can be made online at www.RGT.org, using your unique and confidential examination entry code shown on page 57 of this book.

You will be able to pay the entry fee by credit or debit card at a secure payment page on the RGT website.

Once you have entered online, you should sign this form overleaf. **You must bring this signed form to your exam and hand it to the examiner in order to be admitted to the exam room.**

If NOT entering online, please complete BOTH sides of this form and return to the address overleaf.

SESSION (Spring/Summer/Winter): _____   YEAR: _____

Dates/times NOT available: _____

Note: Only name *specific* dates (and times on those dates) when it would be <u>absolutely impossible</u> for you to attend due to important prior commitments (such as pre-booked overseas travel) which cannot be cancelled. We will then endeavour to avoid scheduling an exam session in your area on those dates. In fairness to all other candidates in your area, **only list dates on which it would be impossible for you to attend.** An entry form that blocks out unreasonable periods may be returned. (Exams may be held on any day of the week including, but not exclusively, weekends. Exams may be held within or outside of the school term.)

Candidate Details: *Please write as clearly as possible using BLOCK CAPITALS*

Candidate Name (as to appear on certificate): _____

Address: _____

_____ Postcode: _____

Tel. No. (day): _____ (mobile): _____

IMPORTANT: Please take care to write your email address below *as clearly as possible* as your exam entry acknowledgement and your exam appointment details will be sent to this email address.

Email:_____
Where an email address is provided your exam correspondence will be sent by email only, and not by post. This will ensure your exam correspondence will reach you sooner.

Teacher Details *(if applicable)*

Teacher Name (as to appear on certificate): _____

RGT Tutor Code (if applicable):_____

Address: _____

_____ Postcode:_____

Tel. No. (day): _____ (mobile): _____

Email:_____

BASS GUITAR – RGT Official Entry Form

The standard LCM entry form is NOT valid for Bass Guitar exam entries.
Entry to the examination is only possible via this original form.
Photocopies of this form will not be accepted under *any* circumstances.

- Completion of this entry form is an agreement to comply with the current syllabus requirements and conditions of entry published at www.RGT.org. Where candidates are entered for examinations by a teacher, parent or guardian that person hereby takes responsibility that the candidate is entered in accordance with the current syllabus requirements and conditions of entry.

- If you are being taught by an *RGT registered* tutor, please hand this completed form to your tutor and request him/her to administer the entry on your behalf.

- For candidates with special needs, a letter giving details should be attached.

Examination Fee: £_____   Late Entry Fee (if applicable): £_____

Total amount submitted: £_____

Cheques or postal orders should be made payable to Registry of Guitar Tutors.

Details of conditions of entry, entry deadlines and examination fees are obtainable from the RGT website: www.RGT.org

Once an entry has been accepted, entry fees cannot be refunded.

CANDIDATE INFORMATION (UK Candidates only)

In order to meet our obligations in monitoring the implementation of equal opportunities policies, UK candidates are required to supply the information requested below. *The information provided will in no way whatsoever influence the marks awarded during the examination.*

Date of birth: _____ Age: _____ Gender – please circle: male / female

Ethnicity (please enter 2 digit code from chart below): _____ Signed: _____

ETHNIC ORIGIN CLASSIFICATIONS (If you prefer not to say, write '17' in the space above.)

White: **01 British**   **02 Irish**   **03 Other white background**

Mixed: **04 White & black Caribbean**   **05 White & black African**   **06 White & Asian**   **07 Other mixed background**

Asian or Asian British: **08 Indian**   **09 Pakistani**   **10 Bangladeshi**   **11 Other Asian background**

Black or Black British: **12 Caribbean**   **13 African**   **14 Other black background**

Chinese or Other Ethnic Group: **15 Chinese**   **16 Other**   **17 Prefer not to say**

I understand and accept the current syllabus regulations and conditions of entry for this examination as specified on the RGT website.

Signed by candidate (if aged 18 or over) _____ Date _____

If candidate is under 18, this form should be signed by a parent/guardian/teacher (circle which applies):

Signed _____ Name_____ Date_____

UK ENTRIES

See overleaf for details of how to enter online OR return this form to:
Registry of Guitar Tutors, Registry Mews, 11 to 13 Wilton Road, Bexhill-on-Sea, E. Sussex, TN40 1HY
(If you have submitted your entry online do NOT post this form, instead you need to sign it above and hand it to the examiner on the day of your exam.)
To contact the RGT office telephone 01424 222222 or Email office@RGT.org

NON-UK ENTRIES

To locate the address within your country that entry forms should be sent to, and to view exam fees in your currency, visit the RGT website **www.RGT.org** and navigate to the 'RGT Worldwide' section.